A

STONE'S

THROW

FROM

CRAY

MICHELLE

ALEXANDER

PRAISE FOR *C R A Y*

"In these challenging times, I'm grateful for these lessons of love and hope. Each poem is an altar, an offering, a prayer tracing my steps back to the hanging wisteria. These poems sing, sizzle, dance, and knock you over without a word of apology, then without warning, they reach out an arm to grab you. Enter this bright garden of words at your own risk…Wise! Stunning! Essential!"

CHERYL BOYCE-TAYLOR, AUTHOR OF *THE LIMITLESS HEART*

"These are powerful and jagged poems, offering no false consolation as it tracks and survives the wreckage of racism and all that is meant by coming apart. Nearly every poem is in memory of someone lost or whose persistence remains unmarked. There is always another in the space of the poem, a form of connection in the midst of a loss now centuries old, but also precisely now. Michelle Alexander's language takes risks but that is only because life itself has been risked, repeatedly, and also now. No 'I' stays at one with oneself under such conditions but there is company among those who have come apart, whose lives can be addressed and renamed. This writing is beautiful and saves no one from the difficulty of its truth."

JUDITH BUTLER

"No easy epiphanies, no evasions, in Michelle Alexander's *A Stone's Throw from C r a y*. Summoning what Derek Walcott has described as 'epic memory,' Alexander transforms 'a past-present that is penal / and aching' into innovative lyric, visual, and sonic poems that re-envision, with hope, our distressing historical moment. 'We've begun / a first song that sings of us,' she writes, 'an Orpheus blackening.' This book exemplifies what poetry does best—staring fiercely into the unspeakable in order to speak a new, redemptive world into existence."

TONY TRIGILIO, AUTHOR OF *THE PUNISHMENT BOOK*

"To labor toward light, one must believe that it exists. Each poem in Alexander's debut is a body working toward light, which reveals, burns, illumines, leads, and destroys, but none can thrive without it. Enter here with courage, this stone's throw from cray. And understand, as Alexander writes, that liberation hangs on attempts."

CM BURROUGHS, AUTHOR OF *MASTER SUFFERING* AND *THE VITAL SYSTEM*

newamericanpress
✳
Milwaukee, Wisconsin

A Stone's Throw from C r a y
© 2025 BY MICHELLE ALEXANDER

Printed in the United States of America
ISBN 978-1-941561-43-0

Cover Art, "Within" by Deborah Alexander
Cover + Book Design by Angelo Maneage

For ordering information, please contact:
INGRAM BOOK GROUP
ONE INGRAM BLVD.
LA VERGNE, TN 37086
(800) 937-8000
ORDERS@INGRAMBOOK.COM

For media and event inquiries, please visit:
WWW.NEWAMERICANPRESS.COM

PROUD MEMBER
[clmp]

This collection goes out to and stems from Little One, V, Sebo, and Auntie L. Rest easy. And to Madeline Alexander, like a love supreme.

A

STONE'S

THROW

FROM

CRAY

CONTENTS

Arms Slurring Into Words

An Orpheus blackening.

Having Touched the Water Ourselves...

Even After the End of Ur Days

Keep Going, Spirit Task

Y(our) Hungry Chords, Bent, As They Are, On Escape

::

"The truth is that colonization, in its very essence, already appeared to be a great purveyor of the psychiatric hospital"

THE WRETCHED OF THE EARTH, FANON

"He had not been notified they would be coming, but K. sat in a chair near the door, dressed in black as they were, and slowly put on new gloves which stretched tightly over his fingers and behaved as if he were expecting visitors. He immediately stood up and looked at the gentlemen inquisitively. 'You've come for me then, have you?'"

THE TRIAL, KAFKA

Arms Slurring Into Words

POST-EPISODE PSYCHIATRIC WARD

I know tonight's sleep / will scrounge for itself I'm tempted / to shake the stars so like mangoes / they'd fall from their trees And you being / free could collect them But / other sights crave / articulation so I hush myself / *not now* / *not now* / *not now* Rather I look / after the socks given to me / adorning my feet / which pace the fetid hallway / I pass the rooms / without locking doors / The fabric is loose / and the rubber grips on my soles stick / to the floor Each / step holds out its resisting / squeak as if guided / by a fermata Alone / but for the night nurse / He allows me to squander / this emptiness / before it explodes / with freshly risen heads / He is not one / for questions *Do you know* / *why you are here*

It is a powerful / question On three occasions / I have failed it / I told them *these questions* / *are the questions of fuck yak* But now / it holds its breath / Now crayon drawings / by others / flame / in a finger of light above / the clock Each drawing / insinuates / some history of release *You aren't* / *in jail* Agamemnon promises the static / from the phone / alighting on my ribs[1] While the outdoors / is a promise kept / behind thick glass Reserved / for an hour a day / The palms of my hands / smell like aluminum / cans from the meds *Do you know why you are here*

As I walk I drown / I drown in a wedding white / eyelet dress / sewn with black / No / today it looks blue / feels paper-thin / So I move / my name in my mouth as / sea-glass / tumbled smooth Iphigenia / All the whispering screwing itself shut / as a jar of fireflies / Nothing says *There glints* / *a knife* / *an altar at the end of things anymore* / *Do you know why you are here*

---

[1] Trajectory and image inspired by Warsan Shire's poem, "Bless the Camels."

NOTHING BUT   AN ACHE

If only I could resist
tracing my steps back
to the hanging wisteria
at Contento—

a Peruvian restaurant—
    which suspends its soft purple
        most disarmingly
        amidst the din
            and dinge of this
New York street.

I thought myself in love.
—

Two years ago,
I saw their black star eyes
fulgurating like ciphers.
—

    As I floated in the bathtub,
wearing a veil of wings, their layers wetted with water
        and the oil-based essence
            of languid flowers.

I called for my cousin's ashes,
        the very grains of Time,
to sit beside me. For time was nothing
        but an ache suffusing the waters
      where I bathed. With   in

    my psychosis, I confused
myself with a many-winged
Seraph, jubilantly   feathered
and singing of God's glories.   Soon to be married
to St. Sebastian, in a dead white dress, a red light
fringing my hair with allegory. I could hear
my heaven-spun bridesmaids
talking nonsense
                through the door.

And among the wisteria,
there hints a joy
of that troubling   yet   luscious   ilk.

AN INVITATION :: COLLECTIVE UNCONSCIOUS

After Leon Damas

Have you ever felt   Memory without the body as haven?
Glacial
as
        gold's wraith fingers
wrapping your neck— A grip like the sight
of wet guillotines, the quick death
I was deprived of. My haunt is frequented by
        raw incantation, let the sheep
skin run hairless,
let the goat skin
slap.
My dears, my visitors from afar, will you make it home
when Memory is a child made out of Morse beats?
Gumbe
        Gumbe
                frame
                    —Drum
                        Rolling
                            from Jamaica to
                                French Guiana
                                    Lathered
                        in
                            Rhythm's
question: Have you ever loved the shark-ringed
island of a devil? Have you ever wandered as the starched
skin of ex-convicts, aged with labor, doubled over—
A destitution that
let salvation   bleed your hands
to hear its ghosts speak.   *Moi, Moi, Moi*[1] echoic Memories.

18   [2] *Moi, Moi, Moi* quotes Leon Damas "Ils sont venus ce soir" [They Came Tonight]

Will I keep you as close to me as my almond trees grown
witchy like a scent's sense of history?
As a prisoner's drum-mouth
broken loose in a fearsome spiral.
We count the nights we dream, in slavers' hands
sewn shut.
Gumbe
    Gumbe
        frame
            —Drum
                Rolling
                    from Jamaica to
                        French Guiana
                            Fresh
                in
                        Rhythm's
gritted teeth. "Green hell,"   revving invisible death,
brutals its own aftertaste.   And Pierced through my ghost nose is a past-present
    that is penal
and aching. When your heart   speaks in these tongues, it has made us
Urgent in every language. Every vowel,   pointing
to here. It won't be   very
                        Long.

BWA KAYIMAN, BOIS CAÏMAN // INTAKE.

The Yanvalou dancer rattles sacredly. She kneels on the ground,
arms slurring into words.
Her shoulders sheen the spell of fire,
            and I inch closer, hemming her until I can see

                                                        the dark specks
            of earring holes nibble through
                        her lobes. *Let us drink in   this blood omen,* my many mouths speak,
            kissed with pig's blood. We are not alone,
                        what's more my brothers and sisters here, Here—
Our thresholds of energy, our plans, have been shaped
    by her movements. She bends herself
            around our very sounds. She says ooooh o we meet: ratata, ta.
We say sleep, our dancer,
    is needless when it wanes under a flood of teeth: ra ta atat ata ta. We've called out where
the thickest leaves enfold us.
            She is taken up with our eyes, and our steps surge
                    to the side without fully committing to the ground.   Corrugated

with exertion,
    her long dress gathers at her hip. Her leg pronates. With the whir
        of her synchronized wrists, she scoops out our interiorities as if to search for seeds.

    Each alone, yet banded we disperse   where the fretwork of the deeper forest warns
against men.

    As a resistance, we will take our own and escape
to the Mapou tree, where anything legion can find us.

Where is our Liberté? We gather. We follow her in
night-shaded
coffee leaves. She snakes away narrowly
among the cane stalks
smelling of calinda near dying, near saved.   Yet still, she will hold us as
her names: Bois Caïman Bwa Kayiman,

on her back, unwavering.

HER CREATION OR EMERGENCY ASSESSMENTS

a poem for two voices

MAGIC
Let us make her know her country
in terms of where forces meet
—circulating goods, the east winds,
the maelstrom afoot,
the clash of world-stage players.

BLACK
Let us make her unafraid
to drink from the rough sea.
Blue-black water caught in
her mouth. The end of
traceable beginnings salting
her throat.

MAGIC
Have we drawn her face?
Let it be a lesson in waiting.
Let us wait for her in the thick of it.

BLACK
Her cheekbones, come
puberty, are the battle.

MAGIC
Soldiers calling before
they fall, compile her body.

BLACK
The ululation bends her
blood, and when we hear the
air pigment with their cry

MAGIC
…her hips are born.
Our stomachs are mutinous
and turning.

> BLACK
> She could wear the dead as her
> curves.

MAGIC
But the cascade of tropical green
and the rough sea, how it disappears the divide
between the living and the animate sky,
makes us think her conscience is clear.

> BLACK
> We feel like she now needs
> our shoulders to punch.

MAGIC
She has yet to put
her fingers to the wind.

> BLACK
> —yet to dial up the ruin
> of this city.

An Orpheus blackening.

REVERSE-CURSE AS ARS POETICA

After Wanda Coleman
In commemoration of those who lost their lives on D-Day.

When opened, space was a ruin, violently forgetting. :: When war traded secrets
with stone, traducing the memory of matter. I came to realize :: how to die
without losing my tender being. (The curse wanted the contrary for me to die
hard, landing with me when I hit the ground).

I had felt being a paratrooper, not the hollow of this curse's hell but a language
for that rich arrhythmia dragging my breath. :: This language jettisoned
syncopations, freeing me borne by heavens as Griswold bags. ::

I threw myself open as a sky twisting :: in cursive. I even tremored belief I didn't
know I had, atmosphered by sweat lancing through my fatigues; my face a depth
camouflaged into the night with cocoa.

I realized ::
it matters not that my body will be eaten down to a precious seed :: it matters
not that the seed of me is being abandoned on Normandy :: sprouting vines of
shrapnel in the sands.

Because I am reversal :: may my mirror be seen through, and may its stain fade.
Its stigmata offered up like forgiveness in the morning :: will form my antonym to
Malice to Malignancy, to this :: M-1 Garand rifle :: that thrashes too, ::

but say these words ::   four times
walking backward if you're able for me. :: An antidote, a ghost whisper ensnaring
a symbolic order filled with bullets, my hands a parachute :: now.

PAPER BAND

Stragglers were smoking what was Dad's in the rose garden. The divorce party lit up Mom's lakeside. This January was a winter feat fete, beaver, mink, coat shine. Our tigerish wounds were velvet, the frothed champagne jubilee of pain, you know. Their adult laughter went up in— a Cigarra, the cicada that frequents cigarrales, the country estates, gardens of Spain. They sing to their own of a colonized Cuba.

Iridescent wing butter, tobaco seed. The sixteenth century unwraps for the colonized like a smoke-swarmed body. Running on empty. Mi amor, robusto my dress box has unhoused Dad's cigars. Wooden in make. Like the sun's echo, La Aroma De Cuba stamps its interior lid. A cartouche plastered with a fair-skinned maiden who prefers to sleep with her eyes open. How the cigar watches rebellion break, licorice/leather 1895. In the stitch of Churchill's mouth, peeled open to the side, billowstruck.

His first taste, embedded with Spanish troops, Cuban guerillas interspersed in his lung blaze. Would we have lit one? Siblings splutter a cloud sorcerers of ash, nuzzled at the front door while the fur-clad parents all thronged in the name of separation. Rationing out breath without the coolness of James Earl Jones, Biggie Smalls, the air so thick with phantoms. There was no wedded hand curled around that cigar, burning its ember. Only a fusillade of puffs. Peering down the box, interns typed letters and old lipsticks, magenta, rust. Its closure conspires accents of cocoa, molasses, earth. House of Don Pepin Garcia— a guest pours a red pout, a cigarra lands: The box is a coffin of bliss.

OUR NET WORTH

After Camille Guthrie

Siblings as gangly as a Blues riff
Brutata &
Pooka sisters
move
our weight in gender, missing teeth, tended weeds
quarter year crises choired
between us against the cool side
of Mom's pillow. We remember,
as forest wolves, our incisors
ached like snow. 4 remain
circa Woodland Terrace.
Our envy of warmth has long been traded for
an iconic back screen door, the end dash
of Dad leaving. & the grip of stars.

Rust, the gate, the knife set
from Peter's
back-kitchen where Pooka Sister turned
hustler and commander. Make it
to North Carolina, there settles in the dust
a coin minted
when Uncle Rob was here, waging laughter
against the sprawling loneliness. 2 tutus.
Mt Fuji littered with dark joy.

We harbor 1 triumphal bang, the cigarette
that burned for weeks,
Sertraline, Clonidine

if not the rose garden, a wristlet of thorns.
Appetites strung out where the color red rises every evening.
Between us, we snuck 1/5th of an
original ark & a drop of flood rain.
Picked by Pop Pop,
4 tomatoes juicier than Biggie proclaimed.
1 renewing fire for each vacation.
An ounce of sage, hands frolicked in mourning
2 minutes before
Brutata left for boarding school.

Kafka's Odradek spooling into a somersaulted legacy
belonging to no fixed address (but ours).
The threads that bind, novel or knot, intersect
into Cy Twombly Pink. Below the scab, we share a
Lake let out for summer. All we left
incomplete, unfinished:
A conflicted look
& converting all this, which
we mistook for language
magic
and signed over to [your name].

TO WISH FOR OURSELVES

For Corbin

*Suzanne Césaire to
her husband Aimé Césaire*

Martinique torrents through you when we sleep
in that other land, in that outside power, which still pierces through
each layer of the language with which we unearth.

You wake refreshed in the flash without
having touched
the glass of water on the bedside
I marvel,

but understand. When no one else is around, and sometimes when there is
we take turns shedding the grip of colonial logic. Dissolving in the hunger.

in a summer fare. Perhaps tonight, there will be "Paysanne" cut
beets on the stove.

The color they exude will not elude the *tightrope of hope*
stretching between us. We wake having touched the water ourselves…

Where the sampan boats float, you and I love, are signifiers
of magic like the word, "liberty," which we want to 'make honest.'

We've begun
a first song that sings of us, an Orpheus blackening.

Now, what reads back our relationship counts us as blue,
blueish, blueish-Green. Through this color, which waters to black,
our critical power anticipates each layer of the language we unearth.

We are hard-won beings. This fact surreals us.
When to savor, is to return as you do. Our indwelling
Power raised on little
time. The changes call us.
No matter how the beginning
chars—
burn in the hollows
     of the mountains
I've said
to which poetry cannibals.
And you, and you, and you
keep the page for me as it molts, as it mirrors,
as it
eats its own.

Having Touched the Water Ourselves...

"FROM EARTH'S ROYAL, DIRTY MOUTH"
OR DUAL DIAGNOSIS

- Tyehimba Jess

From Earth's royal, dirty mouth came the explicit
scar song of teens tied to revolt; came the faded tunes
of swallowed proof. Years deeper
You're asking why you can't
stop, why it is different for you.
Wrestling with primrose thorning your belly. Our prism:
Years become a jellyfish of night colors. And, daylight's brain freeze…
A hijack, shuddered with anticipation of our
near future

It's all for you, this writ, a ghost trap. Because we know to
un-wrong ourselves, to drain the moral coloring like vodka
down the sink, to instill in this universe a memory of
forgiveness. Liquor fireworks through your writhe, as trouble,
one night, you begged me as if in rag's time, to write it down

I'm Sorry, Grand
pa

For the flood of days like chips, for my skin's tightness
and burning, for malnourished, punishing my-
self, and waiting
until the liquor store's closing time
to breathe.

anterior. Hands will have tremored. We've turned to the war of Clenched dreams.
Possessed the verb to hope as it ruptured. Would it have quelled the madding
crowd ricocheting in your body? My prayer wants answers, that the vulgar glass is
not empty; the glass is never poured.

History ... blent ... faced

to discover the ibises

the ruins of sugar estates and abandoned forts. ... Port of Spain, the village road ... already on the sound track, ... real presence ? ... why not the perpetuation of joy ... Couva, Chaguanas, Charley Village? Why was I not ... to the ecstasies of their claim, ... to the feast of Husein. ... to the Chinese Dragon Dance, ... I am only one-eighth ...

that love which took ... the pieces are ... shattered histories, ...

"making" ... the rite that surrenders it ... on the forehead of the past.

[3] Derek Walcott, Nobel Lecture, December 7, 1992

CLEOPATRA'S PATIENTS REACH TOWARD ME, BIPOLAR 1

I arrived as a burnt necropolis.

A barking thing.

         Unruly and limbed.

Read this singe, my Hamsin wind, slow burning and undimmed.

 A mother meager moon hurls herself toward the fray—
An emergency Cleopatra.

       —the fractured night's not over

the fractured night's not over the sky: a killing,

           patients language bossy sinned.

—My speech spindles as a scarab subtly

pinned. Displayed

    intrusive thoughts invade as a conquest, they have kept my eyes skinned.

       I'm grinning wildly...

These patients curl in my spiking air, their hands reach.

Their hands reach.
      Clouds fleece the sky:
       a killing.

Delusions embed deep

                                   as shadowgrams

over which my eyes   skin.

                                 Unruly and limbed.

       A barking   thing, I cry aloud

pinned. Displayed.

                                   My intrusive thoughts invade them: a conquest.

       A mother mania hurls Cleopatra's
patients toward the moon, unabating as
                          this Hamsin wind.

                                   Read this singe. Queen…

                         I arrived

               as a burnt necropolis.

Heedlessly

           Undimmed.

A DANCE WITH FELLOW PATIENT X

She doesn't sit down near the nurses. But comes with me to the center of the floor, a
half-moon of filled chairs

    dappling like light.

      Locus of Locusts. We on fire.

          Two women of wings.

        I followed her movements with my own.

       Fighting chances: a shot residues, dice thrown.

  Her lifted arms in flight. My lifted arms in flight.

         The sign language of lightning.

      Yet, I am incapable of answering the question of if.

What does it mean to follow another along and to the rib?

        Liberation hangs on attempts.

       I find saturation is a language of thirst.

   "Nothing" is a weight of the body, too.

At times, hesitancy charms the trial by fire, as in right before the pill bottle snaps.

  At others, conviction ruled the ceremony. As in shower before light.

          And so I'm learning.

Two women of wings.

      Sitting aloft with all talons curled was a crown.

     When we met, she was a song slithering past sleep.

Now, we're ideographic when our warring smiles levitate.

Our struggle is more bitters than orange, more punk than peace.

Where we got lost, flips slippery as a wish
"Scry," my heroine cried, and the wild listened.

How'd you get here? is but an overworked breath.
Doesn't mean I'm mute, she said wordlessly.

All I know is. I promised, like an engine of history.
My heart is a clash of waves.
Where understanding stands below all irony.
All I can do is trace the war she moves.
Pressure cramps sweetly under my grip, a pain-gilded window.

Play me on repeat, I insist.
She removes all shadow as daggers draw up the side of my face.
Two women bridging the expanse, a pair of monostiched wings.
We dance into survival.
Like summer, I'm a benefactor of untitled desire.

I followed her movements with my own.

Locus of locusts. We on ice.

ILL   FRAGMENTS OF EPIC MEMORY[4] ERASURE 1 & 2 – *LIGHTS OUT BUT NOT BEDTIME.*

the edge   sugar
to which indentured cane cutters were brought   is
                                                          the face
                                                                   afternoon
was a moving,   performed,
Ram
                                                                        like a new
assembling
in red
                                                       colour

                                        armatures of bamboo   like
part of the body of a god,   thighs,   reared,
          burnt as a   The cane structures flashed
sonnet

                                                   nearer the flames to tighten
                                                   the fragmented god who
burnt

Derek Walcott, Nobel Lecture, December 7, 1992   41

Even After the End of Ur Days

LIMINAL TING

[3.]

Who am I if not the riddle's answer?
If inhaling the Atlantic

is to let go.
If inhaling the Atlantic

is to brush against flame, packing heat with immateriality
as if breath. Breath.

Then, as an engine of need

I cave on this Ship to drink.

I know I'll wander the Betweens. Between the haul. Between chains. The belly
intermediate. The zones of bare. The pressure and cramps refuse to talk straight.
Between interiorities, sleep no one.

[2.]

Do we become wick and unbridled?
Fellow Captive, Captain, ShipHand, or Fool?
I exhale and roast an octave, nearly burning your back, my fellow.
All to exhale the Atlantic.
Where there is no metaphysic of escape, a cry becomes gargled. Twisted around
itself
Until it makes another, deeper sound.

And all I can do is set the sun   down below my stomach, near my
knees. Such is sweeter than hot, and my legs brown further.
Eye gestures like waves. Stir the other side of t(h)ings, where the origami'd young
unfold.

[1.]

I will seek the light headfirst.
Quavering full of bounding, you swear
you can see me without seeing me now.
I have been found to go missing easily.

[0.]

Playing hotly, the Captain curves into the desire to capture. What blares from his
mouth, through the ship's floorboards, asks me,
          Why flicker? Why spirit?   Still insisting in the body of a Liminal Ting.
Each is *Breath without bondage*; I fail to think, but I enact.
With your body on top of mine, I grab the Atlantic by its throat.

What would you say were you not bound?

PREVENTATIVE STERILIZATIONS

(~~A Sestina~~ To My Unbirthed)

"I didn't consider all of the female body parts lost in our history…"
–Jasmine Mans

~~Redacted as names,~~ you and I share what blades you
from us. I am insisted as dirty south, my inside breaks out in alarm
~~spotting~~ pinked, lining pieced ~~from my body,~~ and cut ~~just as nakedly,~~ *woah, my loves.*
~~Have not slept but felt paralysis;~~ I have not dawned, ~~but dimmed shading, roil-black.~~
When no refuge harbors enough safety, my waking sleep battles
my mind space shadows my room split sixfold as if ~~kaleidoscoped.~~

~~Hospital corners enfold your mother,~~ even here ~~beautiful as vision. kaleidoscoped,~~
reflected, ~~place in the abyss my strength.~~ My future care of you thrills his scalpel as you
each, bring me closer ~~to you.~~ My foreclosed Daughters, will you brace for these battles?
I will write a letter on my son's knuckles as an alarm.
~~Why, though,~~ to morcellate the fear contained in love? Yes, wrap me raging ~~darkrich,~~
Royal-Black
socket me into this painful fence, an elegy of me? ~~Lament for Me,~~ *Nakedly woah,*
my loves.

Hear me then, stronger as a lunatic, spit me *nakedly woah, my loves.*
Get on my view mirror yourself, kaleidoscoped.
My nurse blunted and said pride was the wound some surgeons carry cauterized burnt
roil-black.
~~Butcher was~~ too kind a word. Wordlessly, when you draw my heart, you
—All silence doesn't tell me. ~~I hollow at bullet point,~~ alarm-
bells hide, and I rise in my dreams at our battles.

There comes incision, too far in, ~~onrush greatest battles~~
~~over how the law~~ of defect, of unfit, ~~scorns~~ *~~nakedly, woah, my loves.~~*
~~My voice~~ was ~~a tide,~~ fighting to shore anaphorically, an alarm.
When it's too selfish to breathe, I reduplicate the kaleidoscoped
geometries. My room walled white, I would find your color, you
writing my names in permanence, both tattoo and tribe rolling out skin-inky Royal I

Your eyes ~~are something that I can feel like~~ your darkly lit pupils dressing me in Roya
I can feel their muddying depth as the *all-good* that battles.
Daring and timidity azuring you
~~with symmetries slowed up, set forth as clearly as~~ *~~nakedly woah, my loves,~~*
wielding radiance like you foresee my shadow's need for counterweights, kaleidoscope
~~Will you luculently~~ join this darksome beat~~ing of alarm?~~

If I glide deeper than ever. If I alarm
your ricochet pieces. I am sorry. Sometimes, I shatter, bleaker than roil-black.
Will you still remain with me? Kaleidoscoped
as if the ruined, the mess, also battles
nakedly woah, my loves.
When there is no future (you)—

There are Days of sharp battles.

SAINT SEBASTIAN (META)TENDED BY SAINT IRENE

After Georges de La Tour

If to be dead is to be dreaming (of godlike favor): You metaphysically rise.

At the table we share, as old friends, u begin to resemble ur ... Father. No, not ur Father per se, but His handwriting. The cursive of ur nose is His. Under my candle, u grow loud as a shadow, then a sharp quiet. We both have greens to eat; yours are with vinegar, mine from the wok. Even though we are friends, and u are dead, there is a feeling like I've been meaning to kiss u nastily. And then there is ur face, the fragments of arrows (*the only thing that move me— excuse me*).

Ain't see nothing, but the flare from the talons fly: With the poignancy of plagues to defeat, Sebo.

When u end, "Okay, I'll come back." And start out: "I *would* have told my Father..." the words s/crawl up ur arms. U become sainted around ur edges like conversion without regret. "It's just the overdose of zeal," u shrug endlessly, stilling in ur shred of cloth. 'Would haves' play out tenderly for us to rave, with the glow of auras. "I'll never eat again," u declare, and yet another year falls from ur mouth. U dust ur Father's name, a ritual, into a blunt wrap u twirl, gliding it under ur nose.

At the level that u are every dream I can't remember:
>   Would have
>   Would have
>   haven't
we added ur entire left palm (which I would lick): lines of heart, head, fate, and sun to possible but foreclosed futures. "Those lines we can only tell," we say. Not live out, we understand. The dishes are yet to be cleaned. No, they've been scrubbed see-through. Knowing the words to A$AP and Hussle u rap them (to me), thugging lonely as u wash ur hands of soap. My friend, u still got it, even after the end of ur days.

UNBIDDEN MOURNING

in response to John Donne

Birmingham was a place they didn't set out

                                        looking for
                              along their way
to the Great Lake, watchers of the water.

Four girls, skin shades multiple: black with yellow ochre,

                                        raw umber,
                              tobacco, and cognac
                              brown, freckled joy in
                              the light. Pausing
before allium blooms, each *melted and made no noise...*

their figures were running down (near your feet) as

                                        honeyed, as
                              blood in battle.
                              Through the
                              ground,
like the roots of hanging trees, they slid into themselves.

She, on the right, yellow ochre, listened

                                              to the
                              blank space
                              grieving for her
                              in the lavender
                              bursts.

For she had thought, what was piercing sometimes endured

                                                        when
                                                        you
                                                        gave it
                                                        the lid
                                                        of your
                                                        eye or
                                                        the
                                                        drum
                                                        of your
                                                        ear.

And she wasn't wholly thrown back like the girl

                                            on the
                                      left, raw
                                      umber, who
                                      leaped
went so swiftly, a doe dancing on the air. The third,

                                  front and center, tobacco,
deliquesced like the salt that interned Lot's wife,

                                      interleaving as
                                      it did, Thought
                                      and Prayer.

The fourth, cognac, saw the dislocation   of the others and,

                                            like the
                                    syncope in
                                    your favorite
                                    word fell out

with the earth

into the atmosphere. They were gone.

                                        The air overlaid
                                with a past, at first, as
                                unassuming
                    as a downstairs bathroom.

III   FRAGMENTS OF EPIC MEMORY[5]
ERASURE 4B – *INCREASED DOSAGE*

And here they are, all in a single Caribbean city, Port of Spain, the sum of history, Trollope's "non-people". A downtown babel of shop signs and streets, mongrelized, polyglot, **a ferment** without a history, **like heaven.** Because that is what such a city is, in the New World, a writer's **heaven.**

A culture, we all know, is **made by its cities.**

Another first morning home**, impatient for the sunrise – a broken sleep. Darkness** at five, and the **drapes** not worth opening; **then,** in **the sudden light,** a cream-walled, brown-roofed police station bordered with short royal palms, in the colonial style, back of it **frothing** trees and taller palms, a pigeon fluttering into the cover of an eave, a rain-stained block of once-modern apartments, the morning side road into the station without traffic. All part of a surprising peace. This quiet happens with every visit to a city that has deepened itself in me. The flowers and the hills are easy, affection for them predictable; it is the architecture that, for the first morning, disorients. A return from American seductions used to make the traveller feel that something was missing, something was trying to complete itself, like the stained concrete apartments. Pan left along the window and the excrescences rear – a city trying to soar, trying to be **brutal,** like an American city in silhouette, stamped from the same mould **as Columbus** or Des Moines. An assertion of power, its decor

[5] Derek Walcott, Nobel Lecture, December 7, 1992

HEAVY AS LIGHT

It sounds like rain,
the thrash of thunder, the flicker beat of lightning.
That's the lure: to slice time. To slice it before it starts to blacken. It goes like this:
I wait for
Ay to revive. I can nearly lose myself in the downpour
of her laugh,
not simply the weather of heights, but more so a fog rolled out in Sheboygan,
laid down near the lake, which covers her smile
with its hand. Tea drenched   I look around corners
to find
if she'd be
waving to the fishermen in the morning light
her ring wrought crooked
her kindness resting around the eyes, tenderly tearing up,
and Morpheus, the god of dreams,
knowing this, feeds me queen
of night flowers. In the diffracting thunder,
my memory becomes a *frozen shock of glass.*[6]

***

I speak to you of *the splash-lash of lightning that is opening up the corners* of her
old living room—
Don't you see, can't you trace how the light   dispels and recasts   shadows for a
second? Shadows dream chasing black as if it were sweltering, with
the verdant green of hope that she

---

[6] Italicized text sequentially renders Teju Cole, Wanda Coleman, Franz Kafka, and Trevor Hall.

returns. Parting

with sound, injecting

slumbrous
spring.

An injection that streams light's cracks,
dawning across her sofa. And I wish to ask if dispelling
shadows is a heavy or light gesture. If recasting
lostness is possible or wanted.
If dispelling the silhouettes of under-eye circles
is a Kafkan belief. That is a black-mirrored
guillotine, as heavy as
light.

Without knowing this taste, I craved black
as a salve for stretch marks,
which root in my hips.
I thought black tasted of biographies
sharpening their wings. Thought
it double-dipped its meaning and could
speak, stay: a saving grace. But also, (the foreshadowing
walked through
the door like her neighbor) I thought it was
a fumble of absence. Or, at least, the shape
of absence. A bullet hole, an exit wound.
Overdetermined like a dream. And punk-cratered like a moon that is
swimming backstrokes on the   roof
of her mouth, sounding to reassure
me in the most clutch of moments: "I'm not concerned."

***

"I'm not concerned."

"I'm not"—I never thought

What if black is not overgrown for some palettes

but is balanced as ash on wind?

I thought, some brewed black in the kiss of wrists, and this was it. If it prowls closer
to the grit of ordinary people, then

it moves as a backdrop, fireworks swirling panoramically

on 41 South, Ay laughing in delight as if she conjured them herself.

"Spark a match and watch the candle burn,"

crackling from her phone. What is 33, anyhow?   A psalm, a highway, her
years as divine as concoctions, uttering utterly— when I can't sleep, I've driven.

I see her trilling, remixing personas, slurping the grapefruit of her many lives.

And all before I've turned the bend, gliding over its very mess.

***

Whatever I thought that morning, black appeared just under the surface, perhaps

the asphalt of the onramp   to paradise, but mostly its unyielding

taste formed in the frantic continuity   between steps taken—the

black of a room slippery   with a new emptiness, the black of furiously

reading an address to the operator, the black of barely

dragging her body onto the wood floor, the black of failed   revival.

All blackened

when I lost her, sleeping in the Lovesac across from me.

Step, stricken, step, around its grit, we go.

That night skins its knees to
find the burning brightness
of black underneath. No longer a
secret or riddle,
black moves the sky to brighten as a screen but with loss.

***

Perhaps it is more like Komunyakaa's *"we move* like a platoon of silhouettes [...] /
unaware our shadows have untied / from us, wandered off / & gotten lost."
And isn't this green, also black? When
we cease, our shadows play. I can feel us sprawling to the sky
like the flame trees we've grown into. The pyromancy of green feeds us
by hand. Feeds us back
what has been turned black.

Keep Going, *Spirit Task*

CHERYL BOYCE-TAYLOR

Not good on our own
You knew to color us as
ripe as d'innocence of muthafuckas. Knew to
undress the page. Freely
war for the limitless distillation of our Need.
Stack stones cry mango green as lament.
Ocean the hibiscus sweat of thieves.
Break Uzi like tablet of stone.

Roll up to the fearsome ruckus
after it all. We await you happily, a rabble
of applause, a sal(i)vation
of blunt wraps licked clean together.
You've
wrested from the skull:
the fracture
of levity
that pickles in our bones.
So needful.
And we ate your distance
spasmodically the first time. Second,
we would confess
that we had not yet popped off
before there, you, be.

A party crystallizing,
a heat like frisson
speeding beyond sense.

With Flame-blue improv for cheeks, you
bring us to silence.
And everyone is more than
pleased you've arrived in their noiseless quake.
This Yearning we
Feel
She's you.

SUN RA NIGHT MUSIC

Sun Ra's sequins silvered, draping as a vision turned up.
Our Astro-Black genius of 1989 stands

his head enchained in the purple
of this untenable earth.
The fire licks mystically from the belly of the bass.
Saxophones shamble
kettle-drummed
jazzily
before the suit jacket asks,

"What were your early inspirations?"

As they play, Sun Ra's words chill and gather in the air:

I draw from *the creator* and conduct my Arkestra band like a thought

of the impossible. As when the Sunharp seeks its way out to another plane.

I draw from *mythical gods*, I can see them ensnarl

my Arkestra bled grandiose, inspired
with Cosmic tone organs for eyes.
I draw from *real ones.*

My fingers grace the keys
vibrate spatially specialize
Is the audience live?

I draw from *people*

SCORES OF BLACKNESS: STRINGS

i.

Yet he sheds anger about bronzer
fingertips on crisp white doors.
She breaks her silence, "You don't hear me
when I speak"
(in negative refractive indexes).

He shakes his head, "*Gangs* of light."

"Yes," she replies, "A resolution beyond
the difference between us."

She turns into herself, "My Queen,
my Blackness,"
his voice a near whisper
to her now.

ii.

My Blackness is Corrections and Emendations: *All those slaves*
who were baptized are not, in fact, free.
Policeman at the house
looking for me. As much as my Blackness steeps
in the poetics of drapetomania[7] and
iterations of Jackie Brown, it is also joyous
laughter, hands slapping the knee.
The Chorus sings of *not really black* Blackness.
The baseball team, chanting, *going to lynch me a…*
and pointing at me.

---

[7] "Drapetomania" is described by Oxford Reference as a "A form of
mania supposedly affecting slaves in the 19th century, manifested by an
uncontrollable impulse to wander or run away from their white masters,
preventable by regular whipping." It has been noted by the Jim Crow
Museum, stating, "In May, 1851, Dr. Samuel A. Cartwright, a Louisiana
physician, published a paper entitled, "Report On The Diseases and Physical
Peculiarities Of The Negro race." The paper appeared in *The New Orleans*
Medical and Surgical Journal, a reputable scholarly publication […] In his
words: *'Drapetomania is from draptise. A runaway slave is mania mad or crazy.*
It is unknown to our medical authorities, although its diagnostic symptoms be
absconding from service, is well known to our planters and overseers. In noticing
a disease that, therefore, is hitherto classed among the long list of maladies that
man is subject to, it was necessary to have a new term to express it. The cause in
most cases that induces the Negro to run away from service is as much a disease
of the mind as any other species of mental alienation, and much more curable as
a general rule. With the advantages of proper medical advice strictly followed,
this troublesome practice that many Negroes have of running away can be almost
entirely prevented, although the slaves are located on the borders of a free state
within a stone's throw of abolitionists.'

iii.

I call to me the strange intervals, the blue notes of my
Blackness. Like little stones, the memories gather
at my ankles;
my Blackness swims in the waters
of Mulatu Astatke's vibraphonic will.

My Blackness wells Trini-deep when Trumpet
tells us of the crab men off the dark road
that he tries not to hit. How they
scurry before him, teeming in the moonlight.
An island sugars at my fingers.

iv.

As a kid, my Blackness prayed to come back as Hendrix.
When my dad Blackens, his Blackness
masters Chopin anyway. Drink deeply
from her Blackness, Nina Simone.
Is there ever enough Excellence?
My Blackness titrates to a shiver when
it shares the sample *I Got The...*
Labi Siffre.

And when my mind
is untouched,
my Blackness is the rocking chair
with Leemoy, her father's hand
grasping hers.

SCORES OF BLACKNESS: PERCUSSION

v.

One drop rule.

She asked me, *Can you even tan?*
        My Blackness
washes moody makeup rings
around sweatshirt
hoods. Never
the right shade. It warns against
    the metaphoricity
of coffee as skin.

The crack wars of bi-raciality.   Mulatto.

vi.

My Blackness hunts wild sea moss (Jamaican)
Irish. How it weaves into Grandma's dressing
room, knocking perfume bottles and photographs
of Auntie Fung. Medford. Callaloo
with Pumpkin is gorgeously novella (to me).

vii.

My Blackness is retroactively and honorably
named after M.A. of *The New Jim Crow.*
My dad jokes, *I thought you wrote a book*
            and didn't tell anyone. Purloined Blackness.
Oreo
Hustled
and painting,

Tribe Called Quest's *The Low-End*
            Theory cover in a dedicated fury on wooden boards.

My Blackness occludes
connective tissue.

viii.

Pop Pop on one knee
at Selma.

My Blackness is a she-monster and feeling infinite.
She is in the middle of another story:

> The last time 'today is gorgeous' fell
> from my lips   was when I whispered it
> to my Grandmother Elizabeth (aka Rose of Mayaro, neé Leemoy)
> as I combed her hair.
> Put my AirPods into her ears
> so she could take in Beyoncé's visual album, *Lemonade*,
> as I dyed her gray obsidian.

> We sat   before a mirror I had
> manically scratched
> up with a gray and black rock.

> As I sectioned
> her hair,
> I could feel her smile shape
> into a deep agreement.
> As if
> preconditioning segues
> during which Beyoncé
> takes   up Shire's poetry,
> together reinventing
> the transgenerationally
>   scorned
> Black woman.

WHO LOOK AT ME: AN ARS POETICA

For poet-activist June Jordan, of the people(s)

On the one hand, the poem of our Peoples rose from her blue ink.
She translated between different sorts of being overlooked. Smokeless and
double-dutching
rope in the offing, freeing children underneath an oppressive gaze. An electric blue
quietly recalling:
We were mourning veils drawn across the Congo.
We were turning to Lebanon through her *loud callin'*,
Who look at me?
She embraced so many. (Under her bare feet had lain the psychic depth of black lilies).

On the other hand, our rising came from her pencil.
In her backyard, an iron grill served up the fat of twilight.
Would we come for dinner?
Will we be moved to act, too?
Hard sweetness like night, or a boy's g'race. A shapeshifted June flew toward us.
When she strayed in thought, glancing up—we shared in her silence *a fallen blackbird*.
We found her—
and set her into a crested quail dove fluttering of Jamaica. She strove harder. Now, not a
battering of wings, but a ram. Now, not simply sacrifice, but a brave calling out

Either way, she was there among us, imprinted with letters fresh on her face. The ink,
a rain on our skin. The graphite of our legs told us that night brews brackish. And
Tumbling dry,

> *black alive*, we spoke to June (in her sleep) like a
> coming generation.

Italicized words quotations from June Jordan.

SCORES OF BLACKNESS: WOODWINDS

ix.

Slow up's Jacob Banks, O my Blackened heart.

> Queer Blackness.

> finding Chauncey.

When she shies away, my Blackness recites to herself
Warsan Shire's "fruit too ripe to eat."

Mid-hook up, and — calls me the n-word.   Da fuck.

When Frazier named me Queen Miche. Bloom
in my stomach. Red silk prised from the crack
in the sidewalk a la Ross Gay.

*I put twice as many sweet potatoes
as the recipe required* my Blackness announces to a
sparkling room.

x.

My Blackness is *you would make beautiful babies.*

My Blackness
has ridden in a BMW with the top down, the snow
swelling and swirling inside.

Curtis Mayfield, "Superfly" post-it
because dad killed it
surgery after surgery.

xi.

Thelonius Monk's
portrait waxes
like a postcard of ebony keys.
Black Harvest Film Festival,
          perhaps.
She says that it's a "shut up
and play" situation.

Car dancing's resplendence hooks my Blackness.

xii.

My Blackness reverberates
BLAXPLANATION, Colorado.

Logic appeals to equal vulnerability
Or is it the egalitarianism of what bleeds,
when he sings, *Everybody People, Everybody Bleed?*

                              At NYU, she underestimated my Blackness.

                              Listening to my sister, my Blackness
                        quotes Jesse Williams "The thing is though…
                              the thing is that just because we're magic
                              doesn't mean we're not real."

xiii.

Decolonisation sweatshirts, black and yellow.

Next to that church   *is chicken*
Backseat Freestyle.

                    Air-gasping.

The acridity of relaxing hair.

Gam's Black-friendly prayer group in Mississippi.
The KKK cross on her lawn.   My Blackness is her
making a nativity   out of that
                                        burnt cross.

Brutata drunk
on his own supply of Ponche-de-crème/Punch-a-crum

My Blackness would freak an encore.

Y(our) Hungry Chords,

Bent, As They Are, On Escape

AMERICA TAPS PAUL ROBESON ON THE TELEPHONE WITH THE WELSH MINERS

In Oct. 1957, African American Robeson, who was blacklisted as a performer, and whose passport had been withheld by the authorities (due to his Soviet sympathies), sang to Welsh miners in a transatlantic telephone concert exchange.

Illuminate anew how nocturne
   your bass-baritone can become.
                 The distance of ocean, traversed cerulean by a question: *Didn't*
         my Lord deliver
                 Daniel deliver Daniel deliver Daniel
Didn't my Lord deliver Daniel? —
And who is the lion, golden mouth agape?
             Panting: Ours is we, America. Is a paranoia with fangs
      flashing-on as an outrage. A motion incensed when,
as a vibration's silhouette
      you, Robeson, slip past
our border in high fidelity.
         As if you are asking, O America, why?
   We assume the poetic apostrophe,
playing absent, then playing deified—Uncalled yet on the call.
             If not my Lord, then! AMERI—
An' why not-a every man? You bisect through conviction and resound to your
   miners of rescue.
      Each agent of ours, sneaking along submerged repeaters, signals this question.
             At once, we hear silence rising behind you
                 as cocked bow strings,
             twilight swaying

in New York on the tip of your tongue, utterly spent.
The Welsh choir hanging on like tear-streaked laundry—
We hear in that clean crispness: *Every star did disappear*
That blade sculpts
your elixir:
Yes, freedom
shall be
mine! Not a 5 o'clock shadow,
but a clean-shaven moon. As it wavers,
Night performs, and you are a negative theology that shakes
across spirituals
across spirituals as transatlantic as trade,
as entrancing as your hungry chords, bent, as they are, on escape.

TERRY ANDRAE STATE PARK 2023

Your mom mixed glitter,
in with

you.   You
catching as ashes that glint
in the wind, in our clothes,

in our hair.
As if to belatedly spell out
a way to last,

a way of feeling
the falling that cannot be imagined in advance.

LEGENDARY DISORDER

A great fire burns within me,
but no one stops to warm themselves at it,
and passers-by only see a wisp of smoke.- Vincent Van Gogh.

Vincent in raw siena cobalt is I,
curling through a blue devil flame.
Manic gas lamps siphon my faith.
Boards warp elitist
in their curve,
and vermilion, flatness offends.

Manic gas lamps siphon
my faith.
I am caught in the cackle of
the floor.

What's real for me after
seasons folded
into sleepless eyes? The path splits
around The Church at Auvers:
1890 violet hues, 1890 pure
cobalt, 1890
rustic orange.
Gauguin cooking from scratch,
with sweltering hands, I would compel him to
A Wheatfield with Crows
stay
emboldens my depression.
Theo comes up out of pocket,

yellow ocher, chrome yellow, red lake, dark
outlines around chairs. So little to eat.

I am irreverent with my geometry.
"I am irreverent with my geometry.
"Mental or nervous
"Mental or nervous

    fever or madness, I do not know

    quite what to say or how to name it."

    Take a little sip. Absinthe, emerald green,

    cadmium yellow, chrome orange.
    A starlit sky: what gleams
    Sien Hoornik.

    drops and runs down our bodies like sweat. The work of sex Flowers
    of phosphorescence.

in the brown years, potato farmers
were bowled over by the charred

sun.
"To take up living again" isn't
easy,
but I'm not an amateur.

Speech slows, catatonic. I went too far.
Simultaneous contrast. Lay it
side by side color scream.
Slice of the ear. Prussian blue, ultramarine,
lead white,
zinc white, red ocher,
black.

Take a little sip. Absinthe, emerald green,
cadmium yellow, chrome orange.
Sien Hoornik.
Speech slows, catatonic. I went too far.
Simultaneous contrast. Lay it
side by side color scream.
Slice of the ear. Prussian blue, ultramarine,
lead white,
zinc white, red ocher,
black.
Speech slows, catatonic. I went too far.
Simultaneous contrast. Lay it
side by side color scream.
Slice of the ear. Prussian blue, ultramarine,
lead white,
zinc white, red ocher,
black.

THESE SOUNDS FALL INTO MY MIND

"Disco is the mother of house music.
Funk and Soul are her fathers.
Gospel, blues, rock, R and B, and jazz are her godparents.
Hip hop is her brother." -   Marguerite L Harrold,
Chicago House Music:
Culture and Community

1.

My shadow,
the stretch of a slow-burning intro, is
A woman Romani'd. Is
a woman

who Poured herself an Underground.
At her lowest point, she
    Built
    a "Deep Inside" that
    Housed

Epiphanies.

2.

Traveling across state lines— I've exchanged our wheels for August.

Brother, I've known all along summer is a meta-category, and
when I reach inside my chest, I find decades
of hits.

What a trance spiraled out beyond your pupils, slats of mesmerized light
And Fred Again...

Been scraped up in lonely towns, the ache a pantheon of reasons why

I've known the dark of cars.

Been a body calling home.

I think back to you saying, *Home*
When you are grown,
You will be dirtying dark as Magdalene's feet. Sounds to me like a lullaby,
a pacifier laying away the worry that I'd be anything other than who I'm supposed
to
be.

3.

Crumble an outro.

Are we ruins of a forgotten god? criss-cross steps in a landscape

where the verdict
is to candle against a cavernous night
        still trying
to tell Time our rights.

My hand meters every
        breath unrusting an ecstasy.

                We are a subversive kingdom
                fretting the wonders of Frankie Knuckles' blued
        the music loops: a second coming.

Thunder claps too close; our shelter, a Muzic Box.

Recall the brew of salt and tastes of older Rhythms, Four on the Floor
And spells of God condition our crowd. How it is swollen with
Samples and I think of Father Soul's best friend, humming. Keeping me as a
bowl of
"Paradise,"
Mother, Mother In our mix, the night
needs no escape. An endless repetition will
Suffice

Baby Baby

Synchronize.

It is all building, like creation's hush. Like in Nicolas Jaar's solar system,

you won't have to choose between
the aberration of stars ghosting through your wristband, reaching for your hand,
reaching—

    4.

        Sugar, how you listen. Gather everything you need
        to shed, let it fall from you.

I've been drinking
In
Words
    bled into the sound of their shape, like
        Clammer: now a curve, not a chord
            Making moves across   the mezzanine

My Favorite party
bouncer
Violining the edges
knows
the House that houses you.

I return with our
    childhood, A "Hot Lunch Mix"

    the percolation of our tones
Blades the wind

"OUR ROGUE SWAGGER"
- MALIKA BOOKER

I catch myself inside our rogue Swagger, reposing on the kitchen sink at sundown.
Its hands are in my pockets and ready to touch us. Ready
to measure the depth of our legs with its sly-shied desire: lifting,
        swinging us up, shaking where
we were angered loose, near the sage and lemongrass, the darker pots balance.
I feel swagger, the funk sway, giving way to how we spill
            into this hour rowing, rippling, the tide
        smearing the lodestar winking between us. Light scatters across the lapping sea:
        Your husky mind.
        To be spurred on but not spurious, letting go. How palpable our palms are a smolder.
A sweat rolled tautly,
                my cheek pulled,
a bowstring, your lips arrowed, Godsent—piercing   *swaggas*. Shattering us
Whole. Saying "dive" meaning *dove*. The body knows
                to be in its fearless Fidelity is how we love.
And now You have walked with swagger, after, after. To have walked with whatever
saporous grace   has sashayed in our hips. An abundance.
    I can hear this swaggering even
when it slurp-simmers just for me.
Even when it coils in ears foreign
Diving otherwise.

ILL FRAGMENTS OF EPIC MEMORY[8]
ERASURE 4A– ANOTHER STEP

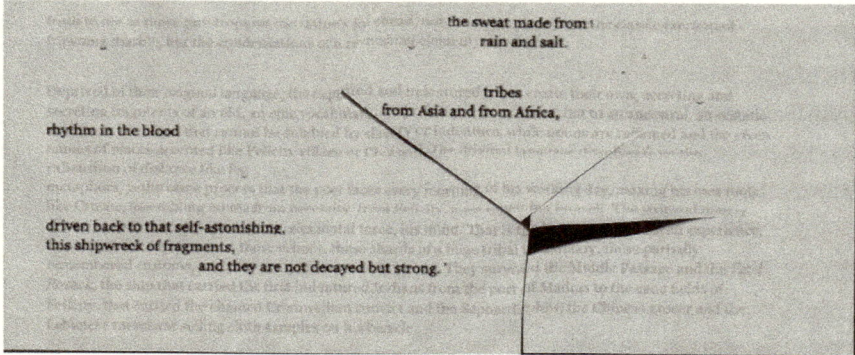

the sweat made from
rain and salt.

tribes
from Asia and from Africa,
rhythm in the blood

driven back to that self-astonishing.
this shipwreck of fragments,
and they are not decayed but strong.

HOPE

Her Chicagoan Daughters

In the grace that falls to us, we will shake,
transfixed, splitting our lips
toward fullness.
Mama, we are Songs, Courage, and Anger
in the mouth of a Chicago train quarrying
through the crashing octaves
to another side —Toward equities. Toward realization.
There is a fervid wind changing, reshaping the way we coast...
Possibility coils around my fingers, a rosary beading symbols: white irises,
    chrysanthemums, questions like:
Will my sister Anger lie peacefully asleep, the train car rocking behind her, dream
    and history? The train loops.
Mama, we've been patient; we will hold you up
to see your reflection within our Chicago: beaches glazed with ice,
our people undimmed. Humboldt, Pilsen, and Englewood,
Resolute as the backbone holding up the freed sky,
As vocal cords bent into raw harmonies,
Our Chicago, an aubade. Just a quarter-block away,
        the human gargoyles fountain, and within their splash,
my sister and I play. Our fingers prune in this cerulean, Mama.
The train loops. We are grown
as a desert that would never kiss food. Our Chicago Footwork is the train of your
dress carried through the
streets.
Before us: 77 communities assemble, their infrastructure
vested, each riot bears the scar of its last goodbye.

Lake surging with light, will, and worthiness. Where the neighborhood went, I will see you, with us as a retinue of blessings, an architect knife exacting our hard and kind. Resistance coloring our cheeks. We are, we are, quarrying through the crashing octaves. In the mouth of a Chicago train
   Courage and Anger,
         Mama, splitting
  our lips.

DRAFTING THE LETTER: WHEN THE CANON BREAKS

After Phillip B. Williams

Dear Evan,

If I were you, c. 2011, and you were me c. 2022; we would huddle in a small bar in Saas-Fee, Switzerland. Our crossed legs would nearly touch. I would tell you what I keep hidden from myself.

The Chicago public library keeps strange hours now. On Sundays, it opens at 1 pm and closes, back in 2012, at the very point when your literary canon breaks. Your joyousness will then have shone Black in the light of Major Jackson's book *Leaving Saturn*. His poetry, this book's crew, will have eaten through your canon with a strange insistence. Almost moth-driven, nocturnally vivacious, working after 3 am. I'm not going to say the book awakens (for you) a literary unfolding of Black excellence —*Leaving Saturn*. But it does. Jackson's book will fissure your white canon with Black names: Sonia Sanchez, Sun Ra, Afaa Micheal Weaver, and Cornelius Eady. It shall play with the poet's wish to speak with the "tongue of God."[9]

That night will have bled its orbit, flowing out the *drain of space*.[10] Sonia Sanchez, a Black poet, and Saturnine satellite, will eclipse a white Holderlin's book *Hyperion*. And in the darkness, the *Hyperion* will grow the smile lines of her poem, "For Tupac Amaru Shakur," into its face. And we will have read, "where is that young man born lonely?/and the ancestors' voices will reply:/he is home tattooing his skin with/white butterflies."[11] Tracing a butterfly, you might even wonder, does it hurt when the canon breaks? The hour of Tupac's tattooing is the hour that strikes when the library closes on Sundays.

It is as serious a Black joy as a lifted depression when the literary canon breaks away from its whiteness. "When space is the place," as Sun Ra reverbs. The shadows in your room will dance around you, purpled at their edges like Prince's rain. The skull of Afro-Futurism will knock against your kitchen wall. You'll mistake it for the heat running through the pipes. But when a collective moan escapes the

---

[9] From Major Jackson's "Blunts"
[10] Language evoked from Ocean Vuong's poem, "Immigrant Haibun."
[11] From Sonia Sanchez's "For Tupac Amaru Shakur."

radiator, you'll take notice. You'll feel the cashmere tendons of your cousin's spirit pulling the wool from your eyes. Threading "Dat is Crazy" between bumps of the bass. Ah, yes, there will be bass when your canon breaks. The ancestors' voices rise: You know, how we do.

It's how the aubade of Black joy is rawness. It's how the cotton crop remembers the songs sung out during its picking. Joyful resistance darkens in the sun, looking sexy. You know, what is the part that the thugs skip? —Washing cousin V's bloodied clothes in lavender water after he passes. —Bringing Grandma to the church. Her saying, if only he'd learned to love himself.

Here we go, asking after the connection between vulnerability and joy. What Phillip B. Williams says he "saw as a child and mistook for love itself."[12] But what of We Real Cool a la hooks, Brooks, Ankita? What rhymes with joy? If not a risk of breaking the exterior. The connection that Julia will have pointed up in your future workshop. This that danger of another sort. This that finger of the DJ, in *Leaving Saturn*, remixing pleasure so its transience will fall on your tongue like a tab of Ecstasy. A la Zadie Smith. A la Tanya. This that ascension in the mundane. So what of rage? An ascension of another sort. Hot and antipodal to Black joy. Damned if I do. Damned if I don't. Rage for the lost joy. For cousin V's: You'll find yourself hacking at a pecan tree with a steel shovel at Grandma's house. With all your might. When the neighbors slow to stare, you'll chase them off.

You got, you got, you got pain for the vanished joy. Cousin V at the beach, screaming in the waves. At the base of the pecan tree, they will have shown up police. Be afraid, but don't show your fear. They'll encircle you, an animal loosed. You'll have been a disturbance, sinking rage into the everyday. —You'll return in a daze to *Leaving Saturn*, which dedicates a poem to Afaa Micheal Weaver. Where Jackson lifts Weaver's hand to his page, "love's whacked our ribs to steel."[13] Steel yourself for joy. Later, Weaver will tell you who sits across the aisle from Black joy. Those Black men "keeping the weeping heads of gods in their eyes."[14]

---

[12]   From Phillip B. Williams' "Black Joy"
[13]   From Major Jackson's "Urban Renewal: ix. To Afaa Michael Weaver"
[14]   From Afaa Michael Weaver's "American Income"

So Black joy's dark night will have you tattooing Malcolm X's "X" on your right arm because his Autobiography is the first text where your sister feels recognized. What will prosper? Is it a promise or a threat? When the library closes, we will know the color of your pain. Its hour will toll the flesh tone of your madness. But also, it will call to your side the panther that stalks Black joy.

Soon, my friend, I'll henna your hands with the cold sweat of the white canon. The ancestors' voices will reply: The sweat falls up our Black hands in retrograde.

Love,

Michelle

THE RETURN

After Tracy K. Smith

At some point, they'll want to know how the ocean floor felt of magma. Cooled and lifting upward between our dark toes. "Like a spit rhyme refraining, our sojourn felt familiar," we'll say to them, "and that sedimented our delight at stepping forward."

They'll wonder if a chord struck for the Silk Cotton trees of Trinidad gone in the swallowing distance.

How it was we walked in concert, motion slowed by the drag of the waters to Africa until awaited Africa was no longer a mere birthmark on our curving, unmarred breasts. Or a condition of fulfillment, but a place from which to rise out of the Atlantic depths.

What's the secret we'll keep for ourselves? They'll want to know that as we rose, glimmering.

We saw how the bubbles haloing around our braided heads licked the surface of the unfathomable.

NOTES

Arms Slurring Into Words

"Post-Episode Psychiatric Ward"

1. Iphigenia and Agamemnon are figures of Ancient Greek mythology. See Aeschylus' *Agamemnon.*

2. "Flame in a finger of light" is a confusion of imagery found in Ocean Vuong's "Trojan."

3. "the static / from the phone / alighting on my ribs" is crafted from language and imagery evoked from Warsan Shire's poem, "Bless the Camels."

"An Invitation :: Collective Unconscious"

1. "An invitation" is inspired in form by "Ils Sont Venus Ce Soir" ("They Came Tonight]") and is shaped by Leon Damas, poet, politician, and a foundational voice of the Négritude movement.

2. Doubling memory and historical suffering, "wet guillotines" is deployed in contradistinction to 'dry guillotine' a term historically in play, "evoking a slow, invisible death that contrasted to the quick, bloody spectacle of a Republican-style execution." See "From Green Hell to Gray Heritage: Ecologies of Color in the Penal Colony" by Sophie Fuggle, 2021.

3. "Memory, a child made out of Morse beats" draws after CM Burrough's "Morse-like sibling; sum of recollections" in "DREAM: AFTER HER BURIAL" of *The Vital System*, 2012.

4. "Green Hell" was a nickname given to France's deadly penal colony in French Guiana.

"Bwa Kayiman, Bois Caïman // Intake"

1. "Bwa Kayiman" is Haitian Creole, and "Bois Caïman" is French; a literal English translation is "alligator wood." At the beginning of the Haitian Revolution, Bwa Kayiman was the first major meeting site for enslaved Black people, where a legendary Vodou ceremony took place and strategies were explicated.

"Her Creation or Emergency Assessments"

1. "Rough sea" and "The end of traceable beginnings," are partial quotations from Dionne Brand's *A Map to the Door of No Return: Notes to Belonging*. The latter's full quotation reads, "In some desolate sense it was the creation place of Blacks in the New World Diaspora at the same time that it signified the end of traceable beginnings."

2. "But the cascade of tropical green" aims to call up and after *Trophic Cascade* by Camille T. Dungy.

An Orpheus blackening.

"Reverse-Curse as Ars Poetica"

1. After Wanda Coleman's "Black-Handed Curse" and toward those reversing curses with the poetry of their lives.

2. In consideration of Ocean Vuong's "Daily Bread" that thinks about color's capacity for remembrance: an ars poetica in itself.

"Our Net Worth"

1. The conception behind Camille Guthrie's "My Net Worth" sparked the offering that is "Our Net Worth."

2. Notorious B.I.G.'s "Juicy" (1994) is a powerful presence in the musico-historical consciousness of Hip Hop.

3. "Kafka's Odradek spooling into somersaulted legacy" refers to the author's "The Cares of a Family Man," where Odradek is an object-creature, as untraceable as in/scrutable, yet nonetheless whose transgenerational survival is imagined almost painfully, in the short tale.

"To Wish for Ourselves"

1. Suzanne Césaire in Daniel Maximin, ed., *The Great Camouflage: Writings of Dissent (1941-1945)* (2012) writes renouncing sentimentality, "Far from rhymes, laments, sea breezes, parrots ... we decree the death of sappy, sentimental folkloric literature. And to hell with hibiscus, frangipani, and bougainvillea. Martinican poetry will be cannibal or it will not be." And, "Here the poets feel their heads capsize, and inhaling the fresh smells of the ravines, they take possession of the wreath of islands ... and they see tropical flames kindled no longer in the heliconia, in the gerberas, in the hibiscus, in the bougainvillea, in the flame trees,

but instead in the hungers, and in the tears, in the hatreds, in the ferocity, that burn in the hollows of the mountains."

2. An Orpheus blackening alludes to Satre's *Black Orpheus*, the English translation states, "'Orphee Noir' appeared originally as the preface to an anthology of African and West Indian poets, edited by Léopold Sédar Senghor (Anthologie de la nouvelle poésie nègre et malgache de langue française: Précédée de Orphée noir)."

Having Touched the Water Ourselves

"'From Earth's royal, dirty mouth' or Dual Diagnosis"

1. "From Earth's royal, dirty mouth" quotes Tyehimba Jess "Blind Boone's Vision" in *Olio*.

"Ill   Fragments of Epic Memory Erasure 3 —Patient History [Pt Hx]"

1. "Ill   Fragments of Epic Memory" is a disordering erasure series that takes up as medium the text Derek Walcott's "The Antilles: Fragments of Epic Memory: the Nobel Lecture" given on December 7th, 1992. The committee described his work as a "poetic oeuvre of great luminosity, sustained by a historical vision, the outcome of a multicultural commitment."

2. "Epic memory" refers to the idea that a subconscious is shared by diasporic peoples spread worldwide. This definition is expanded from its Afro-centric root in Abu Shardow Abarry's "Afrocentric Aesthetics in Selected Harlem Renaissance Poetry" from *Language and Literature in the African Imagination*, edited by Carol Aisha Blackshire-Belay. Perhaps the relation of sharing is structured among/ between diasporic peoples and can draw from the way intellectual Edward Said's "secular humanism" "names possibilities of connection and translation among exiled peoples," as formulated by Judith Butler, in a discussion with Cornel West at Columbia University's "Honoring Edward Said." Even as we continue to be wary of certain blindspots in humanistic endeavors.

3. "Ill" is an erasure of "Antilles," and is meant in its double sense as both sick and cool.

4. The graphic split implicitly attends to critical thinker Avital Ronell's concept of "splutterance" appearing in *Stupidity*, where a critical engagement with Wordsworth unfolds, "In the slasher poems, language is matted to bodies and

affects, as in *Peter Bell*, where the organs, crossing the liver, recall that language in Wordsworth invades the body and drives it to utterance, or in this case to "splutterance" to a figure worn down by painful literality." Perhaps we can translate this painful literality into "spliterature," a constitutive splitting of literature as subject by the multiplicity of languages. This split also lends a visceral cast to "fragment(s)" as process and effect.

"Ill   Fragments of Epic Memory Erasure 1 & 2— Lights Out but Not Bedtime."

1.   See notes for "Ill   Fragment of Epic Memory Erasure 3"

Even After the End of Ur Days

"Preventative Sterilizations (A Sestina To My Unbirthed)"

1.   Historically, Black bodies have been used to further medical and scientific experimentation in the United States. This has occurred into the late twentieth century and beyond. At times, Black women, Indigenous women, and other women of color with mental disorders, were eugenically prognosticated as mentally unfit to reproduce and were sterilized on that basis. For further illumination on reproductive injustice see Volscho, Thomas W. "Sterilization Racism and Pan-Ethnic Disparities of the Past Decade: The Continued Encroachment on Reproductive Rights." *Wicazo Sa Review*, vol. 25, no. 1, 2010, pp. 17–31. JSTOR, http://www.jstor.org/stable/40891307. Accessed 1 Aug. 2024.

2.   The epigraph, "I didn't consider all of the female body parts lost in our history," that completes itself in "all the names of women unconsidered," is a quotation from Jasmine Mans' "Bodies Lost in History" from *Black Girl, Call Home*.

3.   The emotional tenor of "To My Unbirthed" germinates in "Rage is essential/I carry it like the babies/I can no longer bare" in "For my Comrades" by Cheryl Boyce-Taylor.

4.   "Kaleidoscoped" here invokes its 6-fold construction where, according to *Thresholds of Science* by Charles Romley Alder Wright, "if the mirrors are inclined at 60 degrees, there will be five images visible in addition to the real object, all six being arranged in a six-pointed star" which can, in a certain light, mirror the sestina form's special relation to six with its six repeating words and six-line stanzas.

"Saint Sebastian (Meta)tended by Saint Irene"

1. The title signals George de La Tour's c. 1694 oil-on-canvas painting, "Saint Sebastian Tended by Saint Irene."

2. "(*The only thing that move me- excuse me*)" is a lyric from A$AP Rocky "Excuse Me," 2015.

3. "*Ain't see nothing, but the flare from the talon's fly*" is a lyric from Nipsey Hussle's "Blue Laces 2," 2018.

4. "Okay, I'll come back" represents the last words of rapper Pop Smoke, whose death resulted from gun violence. This ties into the sense of a modern plague.

5. "(Symphonies of) 'would haves' play out tenderly (enough) for us to rave, with the glow of auras" has been syntactically and rhythmically modeled on Ocean Vuong's "Immigrant Haibun," "Little centuries opening just long enough for us to slip through."

"Unbidden Mourning"

1. "Unbidden Mourning," as the title and poem, is in an underwater conversation, so to speak, with John Donne's "A Valediction: Forbidding Mourning" and functions elegiacally for Denise McNair, Cynthia Wesley, Carole Robertson, Addie Mae Collins: the four girls murdered in the Birmingham 16th Street Baptist Church bombing of 1963.

"Ill   Fragments of Epic Memory Erasure 4b— Increased Dosage"

1. See notes for "Ill   Fragment of Epic Memory Erasure 3"

Keep Going, Spirit Task

"Cheryl Boyce-Taylor"

1. As the title states, the poem is in honor of Trinidadian poet, Cheryl Boyce Taylor.

"Sun Ra Night Music"

1. "Sun Ra Night Music" is inspired by Sun Ra's interview and Sun Ra and his Arkestra's performance on the show *Night Music* of 1989.

2. "Untenable Earth" excerpts from a quotation of "The specifics of Ra's vision remained hazy, but he seemed to believe that the traumas of history—most notably of American slavery—had made life on Earth untenable" in "How Sun Ra Taught Us to Imagine the Impossible" a *New Yorker* article, 2021 by Hua Hsu.

"Scores of Blackness: Strings"

1. The play of senses at work in the phrase "Scores of Blackness" arose into consciousness partly from a consideration of critical thinker Avital Ronell's *Finitude's Score* and partly from the reflection on *synesthesia* in "Troubling Vision: Performance, Visuality, and Blackness" by Nicole R. Fleetwood.

2. Negative refractive indexes are enabled by the field of metamaterials, which has shaped my consideration of Afro-Futurism.

3. "All those slaves who were baptized are not, in fact, free" was a retelling of the law "an act declaring that baptisme of slaves doth not exempt them from bondage" passed by the national assembly in the session of September 1667 of Virginia's colonial government.

4. "Warns against the metaphoricity of coffee as skin" is a countermelody to "Coffee Colored Coon" as appears in Tyehimba Jess' *Olio*.

"Scores of Blackness: Percussion"

1. "One drop rule," is in reference to the United States principle behind a historico-racial identity category "Black" or "African American" as referencing a person having any Black ancestry. This rule is intended to proliferate hypodescent.

2. Selma, as in the Selma to Montgomery Alabama march, civil rights protests, United States, 1965.

"Who Look At Me: An Ars Poetica"

1. "Who Look At Me" refers to the title of June Jordan's ekphrastic book of poetry (1969). In describing how this book came to be, Jordan wrote, "We do not see those we do not know. And, in a nation suffering fierce hatred, the question, race to race, man to man, and child to child, is WHO LOOK AT ME. *We answer with our lives.* Let the human eye begin an unlimited embrace of human life." Jordan's words continue to resonate today.

2. "*Gender, grief and ash*" is a quotation from June Jordan's poem, "For Alice Walker (a summertime tanka)."

3. "Ram" alludes to Jacques Derrida's contemplation in "Uninterrupted Dialogue: Between Two Infinities, the Poem" in *Research in Phenomenology* (2004).

4. "*Black alive,*" quotes June Jordan's *Who Look at Me*: "I am black alive and looking back at you." It also allusively harmonizes with some of the senses germinating in the title, and concept, *Black Aliveness, or A Poetics of Being* by Kevin Quashie.

"Scores of Blackness: Woodwinds".

1. "Slow up's Jacob Banks" inverts the possessive structure of Jacob Banks's "Slow up" the chorus of which entreats, "Don't grow up on me/ Keep that backstroke in your Afro/ Don't you grow up on me/ Slow up homie/ Don't you grow up on me/ Keep it OG sipping slowly/ Don't you grow up on me/ Slow up homie."

2. "Curtis Mayfield, "Superfly"" refers to Curtis Mayfield's title track of his 1972 album.

3. "Blaxplanation, Colorado" refers to The Blaxplanation program of History Colorado, which explores the stories of Colorado's Black diaspora—outside the context of slavery—with national or international impact. Reclaiming its name from the Blaxploitation genre of the 70s, this program addresses racist and discriminatory understandings of Black life while focusing on the contributions and achievements of the Black community to our society. Created by Dexter Nelson II and Madeline Alexander. 2021-present.

4. *"Everybody People, Everybody Bleed"* refers to Logic's track, "Everybody" in which the chorus line runs, "Everybody people, everybody bleed, everybody need something everybody love, everybody know, how it go."

5. Jesse Williams' quote, "The thing is though… the thing is that just because we're magic doesn't mean we're not real" comes from his acceptance speech when he received BET's Humanitarian Award, 2016.

6. *"Next to that Church   is   chicken"* is a misquotation of Kendrick Lamar's "Backseat Freestyle" "Park it in front of Lueders, next to that Church's chicken."

7. "Air-gasping" invokes by way of wish-image George Floyd's last words, "I can't breathe" because the gasp of air splutters the wish of his survival. Black American, Floyd, forty-six, was murdered by Derek Chauvin, a forty-four-year-old white police officer in 2020 Minneapolis, United States of America.

Y(our) Hungry Chords Bent, As They Are, On Escape

"America Taps Paul Robeson on the Telephone with the Welsh Miners"

1. Paul Robeson (1898-1976), born in Princeton, N.J., U.S. as the son of a former enslaved man. Robeson was a Black activist, scholar, singer, athlete, actor, and lawyer of many political commitments.

2. *"Didn't my Lord deliver ..."* and the subsequent italicized verses are extracted from the spiritual "Didn't My Lord Deliver Daniel?" Robeson sang the spiritual on the transatlantic telephone concert.

3. "Apostrophe" refers to the poetic figure, which functions as "An address to a dead or absent person, or personification as if he or she or they were present," according to The Poetry Foundation's "Glossary of Poetic Terms" 2024.

4. "Repeater" refers here to the repeaters placed underwater, "developed as electronic amplifiers to relay the signals on long-distance cables." Cited in, "Robeson Sings: The First Transatlantic Telephone Cable," Science Museum, 2018.

5. "Negative theology" refers to the idea of a "God, we can know and say only what 'he' is not. Since God is metaphysically anterior to the world of intelligible beings, no predicate deployed within human language is capable of circumscribing him within the limits of signification. In the discourses of negative theology, everything that is said about theos is said under erasure and as cancels itself out, since God is understood to be unnameable, unsayable, and indeed inconceivable" according to the *Encyclopedia of Sciences and Religions* 2013 article by William Franke and Chance Brandon Woods.

"Legendary Disorder"

1. "A great fire burns within me, but no one stops to warm themselves at it, and passers-by only see a wisp of smoke" paraphrases Vincent Van Gogh's letter to Theo Van Gogh, Cuesmes, between Tuesday, June 22, and Thursday, June 24 1880, in Cuesmes, Belgium, where he writes, "Someone has a great fire in his soul and nobody ever comes to warm themselves at it, and passers-by see nothing but a little smoke at the top of the chimney and then go on their way.

2. "Mental or nervous fever or madness, I do not know quite what to say or how to name it" excerpts from Vincent Van Gogh's letter to Paul Gauguin in Arles, Jan 21, 1889.

3. "To take up living again isn't easy" excerpts from Vincent Van Gogh's letter to Paul Signac c. April 10, 1889. The full quotation reads, "But at times it is not easy for me to take up living again, for there remain inner seizures of despair of a pretty large caliber."

"Our Rogue Swagger"

1. "Our Rogue Swagger" is a quote from Malika Booker's poem, "A Parable of Sorts."

"Ill   Fragments of Epic Memory Erasure 4a— Another Step"

1. See notes for "Ill   Fragment of Epic Memory Erasure 3"
2. "This shipwreck of fragments / and they are not decayed but strong," could be read as sharing an affinity with early German Romantic thought in the history of literary forms insofar as the Romantics take the fragment to not signify the prevailing (historical) notion of residualness but "to bring out the radical atotality of writing" as Rodolphe Gasché writes, in "Ideality in Fragmentation."

"The Return"

1. "The Return" was inspired by Tracy K. Smith's poem "At Some Point They'll Want To Know" from her collection *Life on Mars*, 2011 and the diasporic legend articulated in Dionne Brand's *A Map to the Door of No Return: Notes to Belonging*, 2001.

ACKNOWLEDGMENTS

Some rosemary for good memories; thank you to the editors of the following publications, in which these poems, albeit at times in earlier versions, have appeared:

She Takes a Machete as if She Knows Everything. This chapbook includes: "Scores of Blackness: Strings, Percussion, Woodwinds," "Post-Episode Psychiatric Ward," "Sun Ra Night Music" "Legendary Disorder," "The Return" "Bwa Kayiman, Bois Caïman," and "Nothing But an Ache." (Bottlecap Press, 2023)

"Saint Sebastian (Meta)tended by Saint Irene," as well as "Paper Band" (Spring 2024), "Unbidden Mourning" (*Allium: A Journal of Poetry & Prose*, Fall 2024).

"Drafting the Letter: When the Canon Breaks." (*Salt Hill*, 2023)

"Ode to the Rap Game," and "America Taps Paul Robeson on the Telephone with the Welsh Miners." (*Obsidian: Literature and Arts in the African Diaspora*, forthcoming)."

"Our Net Worth" (*Third Coast*, forthcoming).

"Our Rogue Swagger" (*Epiphany: A Literary Journal*, Fall/Winter 2024)

"Reverse-Curse as Ars Poetica" and "From Earth's Royal, Dirty Mouth" or Dual Diagnosis" (*Puerto Del Sol,* September 2024)

"To Wish for Ourselves" (*Sine Qua Non,* forthcoming)

"These Sounds Fall into My Mind" (*Oxford Poetry*, forthcoming)

"Hope" was commissioned by 2GenPen Trust, LLC.

I am grateful to my MFA cohort at Columbia College Chicago, especially Ankita Sadarjoshi, for your encouragement and trench-warfare tactics in getting these poems to their best versions. Thank you to the Nathan Breitling Poetry Fellowship for enabling me to work on these poems.

A special thanks to CM Burroughs for the cultural and personal reckonings, realizations, and draft work that shaped this manuscript.

Thank you to Tony Trigilio for your reading, to David Trinidad for your promptings. And to my cohort at The European Graduate School for suffering my mayhem, and seeing me through to the other side. Thank you to Avital Ronell and Judith Butler for inspiring me through tough years.

A generous thanks to New American Press and Nikki Wallschlaeger for selecting this manuscript and endeavoring to give it a vibrant existence. Thank you to Deborah Alexander and Angelo Maneage for the cover.

My gratitude sets the air astir around Roger Reeves for selecting "America Taps Paul Robeson on the Telephone with the Welsh Miners" and "Cheryl Boyce-Taylor" for the 2024 Furious Flower Prize. Thank you to Dr. Joanne Gabbin and Lauren K. Alleyne for your welcoming grace.

Thank you to the CC and Kat for your trenchant belief, the Odyssey Project, *Unwoven Literary & Arts Magazine* for your support and celebration, and my family for everything.

MICHELLE ALEXANDER

is an American-Trinidadian poet, creative nonfiction writer, and interdisciplinary practitioner. She graduated from New York University Gallatin School of Individualized Study, receiving the Herbert Rubin Prize in Poetry, and holds an MFA from Columbia College Chicago, where she was a Nathan Breitling Poetry Fellow. She has served as a Poet in Residence for the Chicago Poetry Center and as a Visiting Teaching Artist for the Poetry Foundation's "Forms and Features" series. She is the recipient of the Furious Flower 2024 Poetry Prize and a co-founder + Director of Interdisciplinary Arts at Unwoven Literary & Arts Magazine. Her poetry collection, *A Stone's Throw from C r a y*, the New American Prize winner (2024), was a finalist for The National Poetry Series, The Word Works Competition: Washington Prize, The 42 Miles Prize, and The Lightscatter Prize. Michelle is also the winner of Breakwater Review's 2025 Peseroff Poetry Prize.